In the culinary world, "fusion" is the blending and merging of different traditions and elements of different cultures and regions. While these recipes are not designed to be authentic to any region, the dishes are created to celebrate diversity, embracing change, and trying something different. Every ingredient is easy to find in a grocery store and can be substituted with store bought pre made items should you wish to cut cooking times or use items you and your family love already! I hope you enjoy reading and trying these recipes as much as I enjoyed creating this book and reliving some of my fondest memories. If you have a memory to share about how food and dining experiences have changed your life, please share. Food should be about more than what is in front of you on a plate.

Happy cooking!

Randy Mulder

Randy Mulder

D1568567

Contents

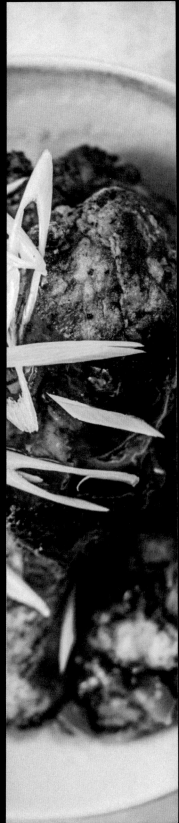

THE GRILLED CHEESE AND TOMATO SOUP

I can't think of a time when bread and cheese has not been paired together. Whether it be enjoying some crackers, cheese, and wine or enjoying a fresh baguette with sliced cheese, this comfort food has been a part of every culture. In recent times, mankind has cooked bread and cheese together making an ultimate pairing. Ever heard of giving a loaf of bread as a gift for a new home buyer? It is so that they may never know hunger. The term "breaking bread" goes back to sharing a meal with someone and tearing off those small pieces to ensure everyone is fed. Why not "break bread" and make one of the most iconic dishes for feeling at home?

The grilled cheese is one of my personal favorite comfort foods on a rainy day. When you're thinking of home and stuck inside, this dish is one of the quickest to make and the ingredients are almost always in your home. Add some of the proper cooking techniques and you enter the realm of bliss. The crunch of a freshly toasted slice of bread paired with the melting of different flavors of cheese is virtually unstoppable. Slide in a side of hearty tomato soup you have a great tradition that families have enjoyed over and over and we will pass down to your own families.

THE AMERICAN GRILLED CHEESE W/ TOMATO SOUP

INGREDIENTS

FOR THE GRILLED CHEESE
2 Slices French read, white, or
sourdough bread
1 oz fresh mozzarella cheese
2 tbsp parmesan cheese
2 slices sharp cheddar
1 tbsp butter softened

FOR THE SOUP
1 can Italian whole tomato in juice
1 cup heavy whipping cream
1 cup chicken or vegetable stock
2 tbsp crushed garlic
1 medium onion diced
¼ tsp celery seed
2 tbsp dried basil
1 tbsp dried oregano
1 ½ tsp kosher salt
 2 tsp ground black pepper
1 tbsp extra virgin olive oil

PROCESS

In a medium sauce pot on medium heat, add olive oil, crushed garlic and diced onion. Saute the onion and garlic until it becomes translucent and a caramelization starts to form on the bottom of the pan.

Add the chicken stock whole tomatoes, basil, oregano, and celery seed and simmer for approximately 20 minutes.

Using a blender or hand mixer, blend all ingredients together. Return blended ingredients back to the pot. Add whipping cream salt and pepper and continue to simmer until consistency is to liking. Additional seasoning may be required.

While soup is simmering on a low heat, warm up a cast iron pan, griddle, or pan of choosing on a medium low heat. On one side of each slice of bread, spread a thin layer of softened butter on the slice of bread. On the opposite side, lay out in an uneven amount the 3 cheeses. This will allow the 3 cheeses to blend together while melting.

Place your remaining butter in your hot pan to melt and add your buttered side of each slice of bread to the pan. Make sure to lift, slide, and move your toasting bread throughout the cheese melting process to brown the bread to the crisp consistency that you would like. When the cheese has been melted, combine the slices of bread together to make your homestyle grilled cheese and serve it side by side with your tomato soup.

SPANISH FUSED GRILLED MANCHEGO, PALACIOS CHORIZO AND GAZPACHO

INGREDIENTS

FOR THE GRILLED CHEESE
1 Baguette Sliced in half lengthwise and ends cut (save the ends)
2 oz shredded Manchego cheese
1.5 oz thin sliced Spanish or Palacios Chorizo
1 tbsp butter softened

FOR THE GAZPACHO
1 can whole tomato in juice
2 oz baguette ends
2 tbsp crushed garlic
1 oz sherry vinegar
2 tsp truffle olive oil
1 oz green bell pepper
1 oz cucumber
1 tsp kosher salt
1 tsp black pepper

PROCESS

In a blender take all of the gazpacho ingredients, minus the truffle oil, and blend to a smooth consistency. Once fully blended, refrigerate until ready. When serving, garnish with a small amount of truffle oil and your garnish of choice

For the Grilled Cheese, follow the same processes as the original Grilled Cheese. The Palacios Chorizo is a cured meat and will blend well with the shredded Manchego.

FRENCH FUSED CROQUE MADAME W/ TOMATO BISQUE

INGREDIENTS

FOR THE CROQUE MADAME
3 slices thick sourdough bread
2 oz béchamel sauce (found in
supplemental recipes)
3 slices ham
3 oz shredded gruyere cheese
2 tbsp butter softened
1 egg

FOR THE SOUP
1 can Italian whole tomato in juice
1 cup heavy whipping cream
1 cup chicken or vegetable stock
2 tbsp crushed garlic
1 medium onion diced
¼ tsp celery seed
2 tbsp dried basil
1 tbsp dried oregano
1 ½ tsp kosher salt
2 tsp ground black pepper
1 tbsp extra virgin olive oil

PROCESS

Follow the same grilled cheese process as our
original recipe, but add sliced ham to melt with
the cheese. Upon completion of the sandwich
cook one egg sunny side up. Apply over the
top of the sandwich, béchamel sauce followed
by the sunny side up egg.

TRIPLE ITALIAN CHEESE AND PESTO W/ MINESTRONE

INGREDIENTS

FOR THE GRILLED CHEESE
1 Italian Baguette
1 oz Fresh Mozzarella
1 oz Pecorino Cheese Shredded
1 oz Fontina Cheese
1 oz Pesto (found in Supplemental Recipes)
2 tbsp butter softened

MINESTRONE
2 tbsp olive oil
1 medium onion diced
1 carrot diced
1 rib celery diced
2 cup tomato juice
1 cup vegetable stock
2 tbsp chopped garlic
1 large russet potato diced
1 tsp dried thyme
1 tsp dried oregano
1 can diced tomato in juice
1 tsp red pepper flake
1 can cannellini beans (drained)
1 cup chopped spinach
1 cup cooked orecchiette or elbow pasta
1 tsp kosher salt
1 tsp black pepper

PROCESS

In a large saucepot heat olive oil on a medium high heat. Add diced onion, carrot, celery, and garlic. Brown until a slight caramelization forms on the bottom of the pan.

Add tomato juice, vegetable stock, diced tomato, potato, thyme, and oregano. Simmer until potatoes have softened. Once softened, add all remaining ingredients and simmer for approximately 5 minutes. Serve with pecorino garnish.

For the grilled cheese follow the same instructions as original Grilled Cheese Recipe.

CHAPTER TWO

PIZZA

Nothing says comfort food like pizza. No matter where you go, it is one of those dishes that you can fall back on in a pinch. "What are we gonna do for dinner?" "We got to the hotel late, what should we eat?" "It's game night, what should we get?" A perfect answer to these questions. . . pizza.

One of my fondest memories of pizza is Christmas Eve. Every Christmas Eve, my family has a tradition of making our own pizzas. My mom would make sure to go and grab every ingredient we wanted and each of us made our own pizzas. Sometimes it turned into a competition and who's "pie" got eaten first, but that is what the holidays are about, right? So why does everyone love pizza? It's the perfect combination of sweet, savory, and complexity. Kids and adults both love it whether you add plenty of toppings or solely cheese. When it comes to pizza, there is no going wrong, which is why it is perfect for fusion dishes. Turn these into a flatbread or thick crust. They work as a family meal, side dish for the big game, or appetizer to share when going out. The options are endless and that's what makes it so desirable.

These recipes hopefully inspire to try new variations and then up the ante. Try to wood or coal fire it. Maybe you have a smoker in your back yard and want to add some smoke flavor. Use different sauces or cheese. The pizza world is your oyster! Go for it.

18

PIZZA MARGHERITA

INGREDIENTS

**FOR THE DOUGH
(MAKES 2 TWELVE INCH PIZZAS)**

1 tsp sugar

1 tbsp yeast

1 ½ cups warm water

1 tbsp olive oil

1 tbsp honey or agave nectar

1 ½ tsp kosher salt

1 ½ C Whole Wheat Flour

2 Cups All Purpose Flour (1/4 cup
reserved to side)

FOR THE PIZZA

1 Portion Pizza Dough

4 oz Marinara or Fresh Tomato Sauce

Fresh Mozzarella

Fresh Basil

PROCESS

In a stand mixer with dough hook attachment, add salt, sugar, yeast and warm water. Mix together on medium speed. With mixer still running, add your honey or agave nectar and olive oil followed by flours. Mix together until the hook attachment creates a semi firm ball of dough. You may need to remove and knead the dough for final mixing. Cover dough and leave to rest for at least 2 hours to rise in a warm location.

Set oven to 425 degrees Fahrenheit.

Once dough has risen, knock down the dough and form the dough with hands or rolling pin to your desired pizza shape. Add your tomato sauce, along with scattered mozzarella and place in oven for approximately 12-15 minutes until cheese is melted and sides and tops are slightly browned.

Remove pizza and let rest. Finely chop basil and add to the top of the pizza while the pizza is still warm and serve .

THAI PIZZA

INGREDIENTS

THAI PEANUT SAUCE
¼ Cup Peanut Butter
¼ Cup Hoisin Sauce
1 tbsp honey or agave nectar
2 tsp rice wine vinegar
½ tsp fresh ginger
2 tbsp spicy sesame oil
1 tbsp water

FOR THE PIZZA
1 portion Pizza Dough
½ cup shredded carrot
¼ cup toasted peanut
½ bean sprout
1 tbsp chopped cilantro
3 green onion chopped
1 ½ cup shredded mozzarella
1 tbsp olive oil

PROCESS

To make sauce, combine all ingredients in a sauce pan and bring to a simmer for approximately 2 minutes. Be careful not to boil. Set to the side.

Set your oven to 425 degrees Fahrenheit. Roll out or toss your dough to desired consistency or size. Place a thin layer of olive oil on dough. Add your peanut sauce, mozzarella and top with peanut, bean sprout, carrot, and green onion. Bake in hot oven for 12 to 15 minutes and pull out to rest. Top with chopped cilantro and serve.

MEXICAN PIZZA

INGREDIENTS

FOR THE PIZZA

1 portion pizza dough
½ can refried beans
½ cup cooked ground beef
½ cup salsa
½ cup shredded mixed cheese
¼ cup pickled jalapeno
¼ cup diced tomato
3 chopped green onions
1 tbsp cotija cheese crumbles
1 tbsp chopped cilantro

PROCESS

Set your oven to 425 degrees Fahrenheit. Roll out or toss your dough to desired consistency or size. Place a thin layer of refried beans on top of dough. Add next layer of salsa, followed by the cooked ground beef. Add mixed cheese to the top and proceed to cover with jalapeno, tomato, and green onion.

Cook in the hot oven for approximately 12 to 15 minutes or until the cheese is fully melted and starting to brown. Pull out of the oven and let rest. Sprinkle the cotija cheese and chopped cilantro over the top, slice, and serve!

CHICKEN FRANCESE

INGREDIENTS

FOR THE PIZZA
1 Portion Pizza Dough
2 Cooked Breaded Chicken Cutlets diced
2 tbsp olive oil
1 cup whole milk ricotta cheese
1 cup shredded mozzarella
1 tsp red pepper flake
1 lemon
3 tbsp chopped garlic

PROCESS

Set your oven to 425 degrees Fahrenheit. Roll out or toss your dough to desired consistency or size. Spread a layer of olive oil on to the pizza dough. Top with shredded mozzarella and dollops of ricotta throughout. Disperse the diced chicken cutlet, red pepper flake, and chopped garlic over the entirety of the pizza.

Cut your lemon in half. Take one half and slice thin circular rings. Disperse these rings across your pizza. With your other lemon half. Squeeze the lemon juice across the pizza.

Bake your pizza for 12 to 15 minutes or until your cheese is melted and browned. Rest for 2 minutes, slice and serve.

CHAPTER THREE

THE MEATBALL

What can be said about the meatball that hasn't been said already. It's perfect for a sub sandwich, appetizer, pasta, or party dish. When I moved to New York City, I couldn't believe how many restaurants had their version of the meatball and sauce. The way you can cook them is endless too! Whether they are baked, steamed, fried, cooked in sauce, we can all agree that we need more meatballs in our life.

You can't just make the meatball; you have to have the sauce or gravy. Slow cook the meatballs in the sauce or simmer in a cast iron the meat absorbs the liquid and flavor and the two compliment each other in the perfect dance. When it comes to fusion, these two flavor profiles must still compliment each other. Much like peanut butter and jelly, meatballs and sauce are two peas in a pod. Try utilizing different flavors that go well together and you will surprise yourself!

The following meatball recipes are sure to start some dialogue. Nothing beats sitting family style passing around the plate of meatballs and boat of sauce. There is a sense of camaraderie found when sharing your food with one another. It becomes an experience instead of an activity.

BEEF & PORK MEATBALLS IN RED SAUCE

INGREDIENTS

FOR THE MEATBALL

1 lb ground beef
1 lb ground pork
2 eggs
½ cup whole milk
¼ cup Italian bread crumbs
1 tbsp olive oil
1 yellow onion minced
¼ cup parsley minced
3 tbsp garlic minced
1 tsp black pepper
1 tbsp kosher salt

1 tsp red pepper flake
1 tsp dried basil
1 tsp dried oregano
2 tbsp grated parmesan reggiano cheese
3 cups tomato sauce

PROCESS

In a mixing bowl soak bread crumbs in the milk for approximately 15 minutes.

While bread crumbs are soaking, heat olive oil in a sauce pan. Saute the garlic and onion until slightly browned and remove.

Take all ingredients and mix thoroughly together in a mixing bowl. Add your soaking bread crumbs and milk and continue to mix. Once all items are combined, refrigerate your mixture for about one hour.

Once meat mixture is cold, wet your hands and form small meatballs about the size of a golf ball on to a cooking tray.

Once all meatballs are made, take a large sauce pan on medium heat and brown on all sides. Once all sides of meatballs are browned, add your tomato sauce and simmer on a low heat for approximately 20 minutes, turning meatballs halfway through. Your meatballs can be served rustic in the same pan or with your favorite pasta!

GREEK LAMB AND FETA IN TZATZIKI

INGREDIENTS

FOR THE MEATBALL
2lb ground lamb
2 eggs
½ cup whole milk
¼ cup plain bread crumbs
1 tbsp olive oil
1 yellow onion minced
¼ cup parsley minced
3 tbsp garlic minced
1 tsp black pepper
1 tbsp kosher salt
1 tsp red pepper flake
1 tsp dried rosemary
1 tsp dried oregano
1 tsp cumin
2 tbsp feta cheese

PROCESS

In a mixing bowl soak bread crumbs in the milk for approximately 15 minutes.

While bread crumbs are soaking, heat olive oil in a sauce pan. Saute the garlic and onion until slightly browned and remove.

Take all ingredients and mix thoroughly together in a mixing bowl. Add your soaking bread crumbs and milk and continue to mix. Once all items are combined, refrigerate your mixture for about one hour.

Once meat mixture is cold, wet your hands and form small meatballs about the size of a golf ball on to a lined cooking tray.

Bake meatballs in an oven preheated to 425 degrees F. Serve with fresh Tzatziki Sauce

40

PINEAPPLE PORK AND BEEF W/ TERIYAKI

INGREDIENTS

FOR THE MEATBALL
1 lb ground beef
1 lb ground pork
2 eggs
¼ cup coconut milk
¼ cup pineapple juice
¼ cup bread crumbs
1 tbsp olive oil
1 yellow onion minced
¼ cup parsley minced
3 tbsp garlic minced
1 tsp black pepper
1 tbsp kosher salt
1 tsp red pepper flake
1 tbsp dried or grated ginger
1 tsp dried oregano
1 tsp white sesame seed

For the Teriyaki Sauce, see supplemental recipe in back of book.

PROCESS

In a mixing bowl soak bread crumbs in the coconut milk and pineapple juice for approximately 15 minutes.

While bread crumbs are soaking, heat olive oil in a sauce pan. Saute the garlic and onion until slightly browned and remove.

Take all ingredients and mix thoroughly together in a mixing bowl. Add your soaking bread crumbs and continue to mix. Once all items are combined refrigerate your mixture for about one hour.

Once meat mixture is cold, wet your hands and form small meatballs about the size of a golf ball on to a lined cooking tray.

Bake meatballs in an oven preheated to 425 degrees F. Glaze with homemade teriyaki sauce and garnish with sesame seed.

SWEDISH STYLE MEATBALL IN GRAVY

INGREDIENTS

FOR THE MEATBALL
1 lb ground beef
1 lb ground pork
2 eggs
½ cup whole milk
¼ cup Italian bread crumbs
1 tbsp olive oil
1 yellow onion minced
¼ cup parsley minced
3 tbsp garlic minced
1 tsp black pepper
1 tbsp kosher salt

FOR THE SWEDISH GRAVY
3 tbsp butter
3 tbsp all purpose flour
2 cups beef stock
1 cup heavy cream
3 tsp Worcestershire sacue
½ cup sour cream
1 tsp kosher salt
1 tsp ground black pepper
1 tbsp chopped parsley

PROCESS

In a mixing bowl soak bread crumbs in the milk for approximately 15 minutes.

While bread crumbs are soaking, heat olive oil in a sauce pan. Saute the garlic and onion until slightly browned and remove.

Take all ingredients and mix thoroughly together in a mixing bowl. Add your soaking bread crumbs and continue to mix. Once all items are combined refrigerate your mixture for about one hour.

Once meat mixture is cold, wet your hands and form small meatballs about the size of a golf ball on to a lined cooking tray. Heat a large pan and brown meatballs on all sides for about 10 minutes. Remove the meatballs.

Add butter and flour to the pan and whisk until mixture is all together and golden brown. Slowly mix in your beef stock, heavy cream, Worcestershire, and sour cream. Use salt and pepper to desired taste. Continue to stir and cook on a medium low heat until all is combined and smooth.

Add in your meatballs and coat. Cook for approximately 5 minutes and serve with chopped parsley as a garnish.

CHAPTER FOUR

MAC AND CHEESE

There can't be a comfort food book and mac and cheese not be in the discussion. Everyone loves mac and cheese. It doesn't matter if you're 8 years old or 80 years old, nothing makes you feel more at home than having a rich and creamy bowl of macaroni and cheese sitting on the table in front of you. The obsession with casserole style dishes isn't lost in macaroni and cheese. There are different cooking methods you can use to achieve the same great product. Make your béchamel sauce and mix it in with your cooked pasta and bake it later, or mix them both hot.

Who says that macaroni and cheese has to be just a bowl of pasta and melted cheese though. In these fusions, this is when dishes can start to get weird and fun. While the concept of mac and cheese is still existing, the flavors can be completely different and bold. From southwestern, northeastern (yes it's lobster mac and cheese served on a roll), and even an Asian twist, they can all find their way to the dinner table. I hope you enjoy the variations of a dish dating back all the way to the 13th century.

TRADITIONAL HOMESTYLE MAC AND CHEESE

INGREDIENTS

MACARONI AND CHEESE
2 cups Bechamel (see supplemental recipes)
1 shredded sharp cheddar cheese
½ cup parmesan cheese
2 cups elbow macaroni pasta cooked
toasted panko (optional)

PROCESS

In a sauce pot heat béchamel sauce to a simmer. Slowly whisk in cheddar cheese and parmesan cheese. Continue whisking until all cheese has melted and sauce is a thick but smooth consistency.

Fold in cooked macaroni pasta and continue to heat until pasta is hot.

Serve pasta in a crock or bowl and top with toasted panko bread crumbs (optional).

SOUTHWEST FIESTA CHICKEN MAC AND CHEESE

INGREDIENTS

FIESTA MAC
2 cups Bechamel (see supplemental recipes)
1 shredded sharp white cheddar cheese
½ cup shredded pepperjack cheese
4 cups penne pasta cooked
¼ cup frozen corn
¼ cup green chile
¼ cup black bean (drained)
1 tbsp chili powder
½ tsp cumin
1 tbsp cilantro chopped
½ tsp mustard powder
Flame Grilled Chicken Breast (optional)

PROCESS

In a sauce pot heat béchamel sauce to a simmer. Slowly whisk in corn, green chile, black bean, cumin, chili powder, and mustard powder.   Add white cheddar and pepperjack cheese. Continue whisking until all cheese has melted and sauce is a thick but smooth consistency.

Fold in cooked macaroni pasta and continue to heat until pasta is hot.

Serve pasta in a crock or bowl and top with favorite seasoned grilled chicken breast for a hearty meal.

MAINE LOBSTER ROLL MAC AND CHEESE

INGREDIENTS

LOBSTER MAC AND CHEESE
2 cups Bechamel Sauce (see
supplemental recipe. Substitute lobster
stock optional)
1 cup shredded fontina cheese
½ cup grated parmesan
1 lb cooked lobster tail
4 cups cooked penne
¼ cup chopped chive
1 tsp smoked paprika
1 tsp butter
2 split top hot dog buns

PROCESS

In a sauce pot heat béchamel sauce to a
simmer. Slowly whisk in fontina and parmesan
cheese. Continue whisking until all cheese
has melted and sauce is a thick but smooth
consistency. Add lobster tail, chive, and
cooked penne.

Hold hot pasta over low eat. While holding,
take butter and spread on the hot dog buns.
Toast hot dog buns. Once finished, place
lobster macaroni and cheese on top of hot
dog bun and add toasted paprika to the top.

STIR FRIED GOCHUJANG MAC AND "CASHEW"

INGREDIENTS

3 cups cooked elbow macaroni pasta
2 tbsp gochujang
1 shallot diced
2 tbsp garlic minced
3 tbsp chopped cashew
2 tsp soy sauce
1 tbsp ketchup
1 lemon
½ tsp ground mustard
1 ½ cup water
1 tbsp cornstarch
1 tsp paprika
1 tsp olive oil
½ cup shredded carrot
½ cup water chestnut
½ cup mushroom
½ cup snap pee
½ cup red bell pepper

PROCESS

In a large sauce pot on medium heat, add olive oil shallot and garlic and cook til browned. Add ketchup, soy sauce, juice of the entire lemon, mustard, water and cornstarch to pan and continue to cook for 3 minutes. Add gochujang and paprika and stir completely. Set sauce aside.

In a separate pan on medium high heat, add olive oil and cook all vegetables. Once vegetables are cooked to desired tenderness, add cooked pasta and gochujang sauce. Once all combined garnish with chopped cashew.

CHAPTER FIVE

FRIED CHICKEN

"Crunchy"

"Juicy"

"Crispy"

"Salty"

The phenomenon of fried chicken is still one of the most baffling concepts to me. How can something so simple, taste so good. Is it the mind playing tricks on us with the crunch combined with a savory smooth and tender chicken breast, thigh, or wing? Is it the sauce we decide to put on it? I like to think it's everything combined into one. Whether you prefer bone in, or bone out, fried chicken is the perfect comfort food.

This chapter is dedicated to the process of a buttermilk soak, or brine. Not only does this help keep the chicken moist and tender, but it also helps your flour mix embrace the outside of your meat to create a crispy outer shell. When you drop it in the deep frying liquid, it is important to ensure you have that batter or fry flour mix covering completely. This will keep oil from penetrating your chicken and will leave it tasting fantastic.

BUTTERMILK SOAKED FRIED CHICKEN

INGREDIENTS

TRADITIONAL FRIED CHICKEN
1 Chicken- separated into 8 pieces
2 cups buttermilk
½ tsp rubbed sage
2 tsp paprika
2 tsp kosher salt
1 tsp white pepper
½ tsp ground thyme
½ tsp dried oregano
½ tsp ground basil
½ tsp cayenne pepper

SEASONED FLOUR
2 cups flour
1 tbsp kosher salt
1 tsp paprika
1 tsp garlic powder
1 tsp onion powder
1 tsp white pepper

For Frying- Use peanut oil or soybean oil

PROCESS

Mix all of the dry ingredients with the buttermilk. After all dry ingredients are mixed add the chicken pieces. Let the chicken soak at least 8 hours. Overnight is best.

Once chicken is ready, heat frying oil to 350 degrees. Coat the chicken fully in the seasoned flour. Make sure the flour is completely dredged.

Drop the chicken in the pan and cook for approximately 10 minutes, then turn the chicken and cook an additional 10 minutes. Use a thermometer to make sure the chicken is to 165 degrees.

Remove the chicken and transfer to a lined baking sheet to rest and allow excess oil to drip off.

FRIED CHICKEN AND BELGIAN WAFFLE
W/ MAPLE SAGE GRAVY

INGREDIENTS

For this recipe, use the traditional Buttermilk Chicken Recipe

BELGIAN WAFFLE RECIPE
2 cups All Purpose Four
1 tbsp baking powder
3 tablespoons granulated sugar
½ tsp salt
1 ½ tsp cinnamon (optional)
2 large eggs-separated
¼ cup vegetable oil
¼ cup melted butter
2 cups whole milk
2 tsp vanilla extract

PROCESS

Prepare a hot waffle iron. In a mixing bowl combine flour, baking powder, sugar, and cinnamon. In a separate bowl, beat the egg yoke with milk, butter and vanilla. Stir this mixture into the dry ingredients. Beat egg whites until a stiff peak forms and then fold into your final batter.

INGREDIENTS

MAPLE SAGE GRAVY
2 tbsp butter
1 medium onion diced
2 tbsp all purpose flour
2 tbsp black pepper
2 tbsp rubbed sage
2 tbsp maple syrup
1 tbsp salt
1 cup heavy cream or whole milk

PROCESS

In a sauce pot, melt butter and sauté diced onion on medium heat. Once onion is cooked, add all purpose flour to form a roux. Cook the roux for approximately 4 minutes until it is golden brown. Slowly whisk in heavy cream and continue stirring. Ensure the roux does not clump. After proper consistency, add salt, black pepper, rubbed sage, and maple syrup. Adjust black pepper and maple syrup for desired sweetness or spice.

70

CHINESE FIVE SPICE FRIED CHICKEN
W/ COCONUT MILK SOAK

INGREDIENTS

COCONUT SOAK FRIED CHICKEN
1 Chicken- separated into 8 pieces
1 ½ cup Coconut Milk
¼ cup rice wine vinegar
2 tsp paprika
2 tsp kosher salt
½ tsp ground fennel
½ tsp ground star anise
½ tsp ground Szechuan peppercon
½ tsp ground clove
½ tsp ground cinnamon

SEASONED FLOUR
2 cups flour
1 tbsp kosher salt
1 tsp paprika
1 tsp garlic powder
1 tsp onion powder
½ tsp ground star anise
½ tsp ground fennel seed
½ tsp sechuan peppercorn
½ tsp ground clove
½ tsp cinnamon stick

PROCESS

Mix all of the dry ingredients with the coconut milk and rice wine vinegar. After all dry ingredients are mixed add the chicken pieces. Let the chicken soak at least 8 hours. Overnight is best.

Once chicken is ready, heat frying oil to 350 degrees. Coat the chicken fully in the seasoned flour. Make sure the chicken is completely dredged.

Drop the chicken in the pan and cook for approximately 10 minutes, then turn the chicken and cook an additional 10 minutes. Use a thermometer to make sure the chicken is to 165 degrees.

Remove the chicken and transfer to a lined baking sheet to rest and allow excess oil to drip off.

Note this recipe has spices that will make the chicken appear darker than the original recipe. This is normal.

75

FILIPINO FRIED CHICKEN ADOBO

This recipe will utilize the traditional method after an initial step of creating a chicken adobo. This method is a traditional dish found in the Philippines with the country twist with a second cook method of frying the chicken.

INGREDIENTS

FOR THE BROTH
2 cups white vinegar
3 tbsp chopped garlic
2 tsp black peppercorn
1 tsp granulated sugar
½ cup soy sauce
½ tsp red pepper flakes
1 ½ cup water

FOR THE SAUCE
3 tbsp lemon juice
2 tbsp agave nectar
2 tbsp fish sauce
1 tablespoon soy sauce
1 jalapeno pepper sliced thin
¼ cup water
1 tsp cornstarch

FRIED CHICKEN
Use traditional fried chicken recipe

PROCESS

In a large pot, add all of the broth ingredients together and bring to a simmer. Add chicken pieces evenly through the pot and allow to simmer for 15-20 minutes, turning halfway throughout the process. Transfer the chicken to a pan and allow to cool. Discard the broth.

At this point follow the same soaking procedures of the original recipe.

While the chicken is soaking, combine the sauce ingredients except for water and cornstarch and bring to a simmer. Combine the water and cornstarch to make a slurry and add to the simmering ingredients. Cook for 3-5 minutes and set to cool.

Follow the remaining frying instructions from the original recipe and toss or cover the fried chicken with the sauce.

CHAPTER SIX

NACHOS

Gather round! Time to celebrate one of my favorite "snacks" and shareable foods; NACHOS! This dish is just a combination of some of the best foods we all love to eat. Chips, cheese, and our favorite type of meat, and this is just the start. Start throwing some pickled jalapeno, home made pico de gallo, guacamole, beans, and more on this and you have another family style comfort dish that will leave the whole table happy and with an empty plate.

Circling back to why I love nachos so much goes back to one of my first memories of eating with my family. I remember my mom making nachos for dinner on weekdays as a child. I had finished my school work and was able to manage playing a little basketball with my brother before my dad came home from work and parked the car blocking the hoop. We would all come inside and right there on the center of the table, my mom made a humongous tray of nachos for us all. In each place setting was a fork and napkin. We would pick at all of the nachos until there was nothing but burnt ends on the side and like any satisfied customer, we would turn our fork over when we were done.

Thinking of experiences like this makes nachos one of my favorite family dishes, not only because of the memories I experienced but thinking of the memories others have experienced as well. Going to a taqueria and ordering some beers with lime or a fishbowl margarita and just enjoying each other's company should be what a shareable dish is all about. Let these recipes instill a shareable experience, not just for the food but for the memories as well.

TEX-MEX NACHOS

INGREDIENTS

1 large bag Tortilla chips
1 lb ground beef
5 tbsp taco seasoning (see supplemental recipe)
¼ cup water
1 can black beans
½ cup shredded cheddar cheese
½ cup shredded pepper jack cheese
1 cup béchamel sauce (see supplemental recipe) or nacho cheese sauce
½ cup diced tomato
1 jalapeno sliced

¼ cup diced red onion
¼ cup guacamole

PROCESS

In a pot, brown the ground beef. Add water and taco seasoning to the ground beef and simmer low.

Set oven to 375 degrees F

While ground beef is cooking, lay a thin layer of tortillas on a line baking tray. Add half of the ground beef taco meat mixture, and lay a ½ cup of béchamel sauce over top. Layer with ¼ cup each of cheddar and pepper jack cheese.

Repeat this step for the remaining beef, béchamel, and cheese. Top with diced tomato, jalapeno, black beans, and red onion.

Place in the oven for 10-12 minutes until all cheese has melted. Add quacamole to the top and serve on the baking tray family style.

IRISH BEER CHEESE NACHOS

INGREDIENTS

1 large bag tortilla chips
1 shredded or diced corned beef
5 tbsp taco seasoning (see supplemental recipe)
3 tbsp 1000 island dressing
½ cup sauerkraut
1 cup beer cheese
1 cup béchamel sauce (see supplemental recipe) or nacho cheese sauce
½ cup diced tomato
1 jalapeno sliced

PROCESS

Follow the same process for this recipe as the traditional nachos but layer the sauerkraut throughout the process. Melt the beer cheese into the béchamel for smooth cheese sauce and bake at 375 degrees F.

Once the top of the nachos has browned, drizzle 1000 island dressing over the top of the nachos and serve family style.

CANADIAN NACHOS (POUTINE)

INGREDIENTS

FOR THE NACHOS
2lb French fries of choosing
1 ½ cups brown gravy
1 ½ cups white cheddar cheese curds

BROWN GRAVY
4 tbsp butter
4 tbsp all purpose flour
20 oz beef broth
1 tsp pepper
1 tsp salt

PROCESS

For the brown gravy make a roux cooking the butter and flour together. Cook for approximately 4 minutes. Add the beef broth and cook until the broth thickens to a gravy consistency. Add the salt and pepper to taste.

Bake or fry the French fries to a crispy texture. After finished, top off the French fries with your home made gravy and cheese curds. The hotter the gravy, the more your cheese curds will melt on to your fries.

ATHENIAN GREEK PITA NACHOS W CHARRED LAMB LOIN

Lamb is one of those ingredients that when served with the right additional ingredients it can explode with flavor.

INGREDIENTS

1 large bag Pita Chips
1 lb ground lamb loin
5 tbsp taco seasoning (see supplemental recipe)
1 tsp ground rosemary
¼ cup water
¼ cup béchamel sauce (see supplemental recipe)
½ cup chopped kalamata olive
½ cup feta cheese
½ cup diced tomato
1 jalapeno sliced
¼ cup diced red onion
¼ cup diced bell pepper
Tzatziki (see supplemental recipe)

PROCESS

In a pot, brown the ground lamb loin. Add water ,ground rosemary, and taco seasoning to the ground lamb and simmer low.

Set oven to 375 degrees F

While ground lamb is cooking, lay a thin layer of pita on a lined baking tray. Add half of the ground lamb taco meat mixture, and lay a ½ cup of béchamel sauce over the top.

Repeat this step for the remaining lamb and béchamel. Top with diced tomato, red onion, bell pepper, olive, and feta cheese.

Place in the oven for 10-12 minutes until all cheese has melted. Add tzatziki to the top and serve on the baking tray family style.

CHAPTER SEVEN

FISH AND CHIPS

Our last comfort food chapter brings us to a fan favorite. The fish and chips. Even before you see fish and chips in front of you, the smell brings you back to the memory of the dish. This olfactory sense stirs up so many feelings that you almost always associate a happy time with a time you ate fish and chips.

For me, this dish reminds me of going to a coastal small town and walking in front of the small local shops, bars and restaurants. The mixed scents of salt water, fried foods, beer, and waffle cone ice cream shops fills my mind. My mouth starts watering thinking about going to a "Fish Fry Friday" or that next trip out on a boat or the dock trying to catch your own dinner. Pair that up with some fresh and golden crisped potatoes, and you have an iconic dish that dates back to the 17th Century.

The next time you sit down at your favorite pub with a pint, enjoy the smells of fried cod, haddock, or whatever your favorite finned friend is,reflect back on some of the times you've shared with friends and family, and look forward to the many times to come.

PUB STYLE ALE FRIED FISH

INGREDIENTS

BEER BATTER
1 cup all purpose flour
1 tbsp garlic powder
1 tbsp onion powder
1 tbsp smoked paprika
1 tbsp black pepper
2 tsp salt
1 egg
1 cup English style beer

FOR FISH AND CHIPS
2 lbs Atlantic Cod cut into 3-4 inch long pieces
2 quarts peanut or soy bean oil
French Fries
Malt Vinegar

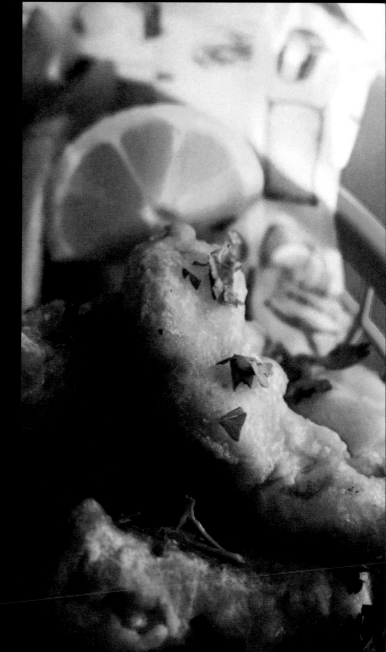

PROCESS

For Beer Batter, mix all dry ingredients in a mixing bowl. Drop egg into the middle and slowly poor the beer while mixing until no longer lumpy. The mix should not be watery and should evenly coat the fish.

Heat oil to 350 degrees. Dip the cod into the beer batter and quickly place in the hot oil. To prevent the fish from sticking to the bottom, slightly swim the fish in the hot oil before fully releasing in to the pot.

When the fish fully floats it is ready to come out of the oil (about 4 minutes). Allow excess oil to run off of the fish and serve with your favorite French fry and malt vinegar.

PACIFIC NORTHWEST RAINBOW TROUT
W/ IDAHO GAUFRETTES

INGREDIENTS

BEER BATTER
1 cup all purpose flour
1 tbsp garlic powder
1 tbsp onion powder
1 tbsp smoked paprika
1 tbsp black pepper
2 tsp salt
1 egg
1 cup Northwest IPA

FOR FISH AND CHIPS
2 lbs Lake Cut Rainbow trout cut into 3-4 inch long pieces
2 quarts peanut or soy bean oil
Idaho Potato (waffle cut on mandolin)

PROCESS

Follow the original recipe, substituting rainbow trout for cod and IPA beer.

For Potato Gaufrettes, thin slice on a mandolin using a waffle cut setting. This will make a nice crinkle cut chip. Change directions of the potato each time you slice. Using the same hot oil, drop the potatoes in and cook. For an extra crispy chip, fry the potato twice.

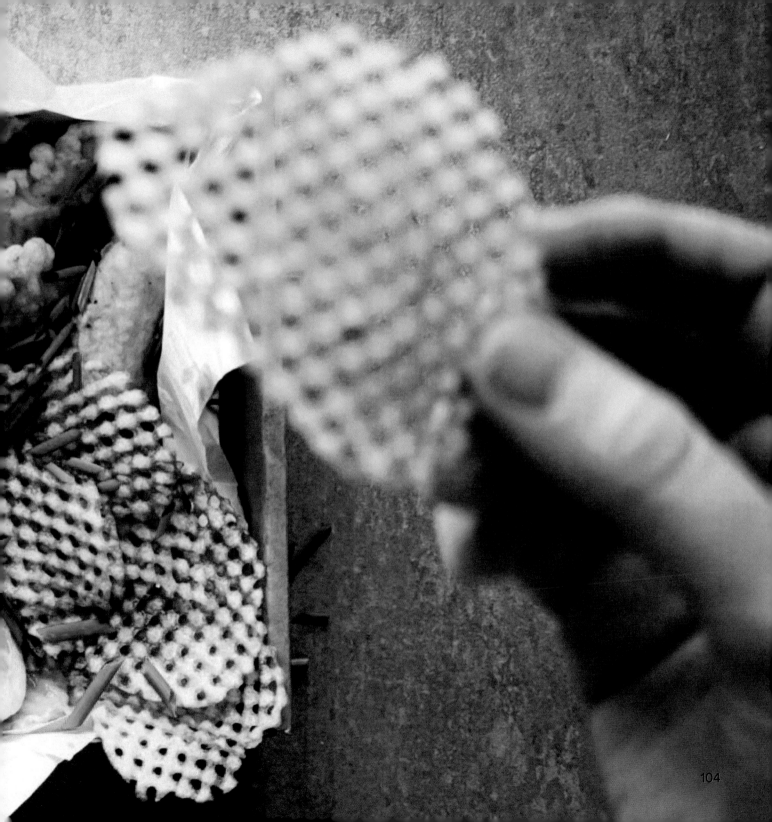

KOREAN FRIED TILAPIA WITH KIMCHI SLAW

INGREDIENTS

For the Fried Tilapia

1 cup all purpose flour sifted
1 egg
1 cup ice cold water
1 tsp salt
2 lbs tilapia cut into 3-4 inch pieces
2 quarts frying oil (soybean or peanut)

Kimchi Slaw
4 green onion chopped
½ cup kimchi
1 tbsp rice vinegar
1 tbsp hot sauce
2 tsp fish sauce
2 tsp hot sesame oil
1 small napa cabbage shredded
¼ cup shredded carrot
¼ cup bean sprout
2 tbsp chopped cilantro

Miso Remoulade
¼ cup Mayonaise
¼ cup white miso paste
1 ½ tbsp rice wine vinegar
1 ½ tbsp mirin
1 tsp ground ginger
1 tsp spicy chili sauce (sambal oelek or sriracha)

PROCESS

For this batter, whisk together the ice cold water and egg. It is important to keep this mixture cold. After this is complete, mix with the flour and salt.

Heat oil to about 350 degrees. Once the oil is hot, dip the tilapia in the batter. Ensure it is fully coated. Cook for approximately 4 minutes and ensure to flip the fish throughout the process.

Pull the cooked fish out of the oil and let rest. Serve with a side of or on top to the kimchi slaw for a fresh take on fish and chips.

NATIVE AMERICAN CHANNEL FISH
W/ PINE NUT CRUST AND GREEN TOMATO FRIES

INGREDIENTS

FOR THE FISH
½ cup pine nuts
½ cup all purpose flour
2 tbsp granulated garlic
1 tbsp onion powder
1 tsp salt
1 tsp pepper
2 lbs catfish cut into 3 oz portions
2 tbsp olive oil

FOR THE GREEN TOMATOES
Green tomato wedges
1 egg
¼ cup whole milk
½ cup all purpose flour
¼ cup cornmeal
¼ cup bread crumbs
1 tsp salt
½ tsp black pepper
Frying oil (soybean or peanut)

PROCESS

Set Oven to 375 degrees F

In a food processer, place all ingredients except for oil and catfish. On a pulse setting, pulse the mix until the pine nut runs coarsely through the flour mix. Once complete, pour to mix into bowl.

Dry off catfish with a paper towel and lightly brush with olive oil. Take the catfish and toss in the pine nut mix. Lay the dredged catfish on a lined baking sheet. Leave space in between each piece of fish. Bake the fish for approximately 12-15 minutes until fish is done and the crust is starting to brown.

For the Tomatoes, whisk the egg and milk together in a bowl. In a separate bowl, mix the cornmeal, bread crumbs, salt and pepper together. Coat each tomato wedge in flour and then proceed to dip in the egg and milk wash, followed by the cornmeal and bread crumb mixture. After this three step process, drop the tomato in hot oil and fry.

Note: The tomatoes can be pan fried in oil and turned halfway through cooking once each side is browned.

110

SUPPLEMENTAL RECIPES

BECHAMEL SAUCE

INGREDIENTS

2 tbsp butter
2 tbsp flour
1 ½ cup whole milk-warm
1 tsp kosher salt
1 tsp black pepper
pinch of nutmeg

PROCESS

Melt butter in a sauce pot. Stir in the flour and cook, while stirring repeatedly. Add warm milk and bring to a simmer. Simmer for 2 to 3 minutes and allow mixture to thicken. Add salt, pepper, and nutmeg. Cool and save for later or combine with cheese to make different styles of cheese sauce.

PIZZA DOUGH

INGREDIENTS

1 tsp sugar
1 tbsp yeast
1 ½ cups warm water
1 tbsp olive oil
1 tbsp honey or agave nectar
1 ½ tsp kosher salt
1 ½ C Whole Wheat Flour
2 Cups All Purpose Flour (1/4 cup reserved to side)

PROCESS

In a stand mixer with dough hook attachment, add salt, sugar, yeast and warm water. Mix together on medium speed. With mixer still running, add your honey or agave nectar and olive oil followed by flours. Mix together until the hook attachment creates a semi firm ball of dough. You may need to remove and knead the dough for final mixing. Cover dough and leave to rest for at least 2 hours to rise in a warm location.

SUPPLEMENTAL RECIPES

PESTO SAUCE

INGREDIENTS

2 cups basil leaves
½ cup parmesan reggiano cheese
½ cup extra virgin olive oil
½ cup pine nuts
3 tbsp fresh garlic
½ tsp salt
½ tsp black pepper

PROCESS

Combine all ingredients into a food processor and process into a slightly chunky consistency.

TZATZIKI SAUCE

INGREDIENTS

1 cucumber peeled
5 garlic cloves
1 tsp champagne vinegar
1 tbsp extra virgin olive oil
2 cup plain greek yogurt
½ tsp white pepper
1 tsp kosher salt
1 tbsp chopped dill

PROCESS

Peel and chop cucumber. Drain the cucumber to squeeze out and remove excess water from the cucumber. Add remaining ingredients to a food processor and mix completely. Keep refrigerated until ready to use.

SUPPLEMENTAL RECIPES

TERIYAKI SAUCE

INGREDIENTS

1 tbsp cornstarch
¼ cup soy sauce
¼ cup brown sugar
1 tsp ginger
1 tsp granulated garlic
2 tbsp honey
2 tbsp water

PROCESS

In a small bowl, mix cornstarch and water. Set aside. In a small sauce pot add all ingredients except for cornstarch. Bring to a simmer. Add cornstarch mix and cook for approximately 2 minutes until sauce thickens.

TACO SEASONING

INGREDIENTS

1 tbsp ancho chili powder
2 tsp ground cumin
2 tsp garlic powder
1 tsp onion powder
1 tsp paprika
1 tsp dried oregano
½ tsp salt
½ tsp black pepper
½ tsp cayenne pepper

Made in the USA
Middletown, DE
03 June 2021